This planner belongs to :

_____

2026

January
S	M	T	W	T	F	S
				1	2	3
4	5	6	7	8	9	10
11	12	13	14	15	16	17
18	19	20	21	22	23	24
25	26	27	28	29	30	31

February
S	M	T	W	T	F	S
1	2	3	4	5	6	7
8	9	10	11	12	13	14
15	16	17	18	19	20	21
22	23	24	25	26	27	28

March
S	M	T	W	T	F	S
1	2	3	4	5	6	7
8	9	10	11	12	13	14
15	16	17	18	19	20	21
22	23	24	25	26	27	28
29	30	31				

April
S	M	T	W	T	F	S
			1	2	3	4
5	6	7	8	9	10	11
12	13	14	15	16	17	18
19	20	21	22	23	24	25
26	27	28	29	30		

May
S	M	T	W	T	F	S
					1	2
3	4	5	6	7	8	9
10	11	12	13	14	15	16
17	18	19	20	21	22	23
24	25	26	27	28	29	30
31						

June
S	M	T	W	T	F	S
	1	2	3	4	5	6
7	8	9	10	11	12	13
14	15	16	17	18	19	20
21	22	23	24	25	26	27
28	29	30				

July
S	M	T	W	T	F	S
			1	2	3	4
5	6	7	8	9	10	11
12	13	14	15	16	17	18
19	20	21	22	23	24	25
26	27	28	29	30	31	

August
S	M	T	W	T	F	S
						1
2	3	4	5	6	7	8
9	10	11	12	13	14	15
16	17	18	19	20	21	22
23	24	25	26	27	28	29
30	31					

September
S	M	T	W	T	F	S
		1	2	3	4	5
6	7	8	9	10	11	12
13	14	15	16	17	18	19
20	21	22	23	24	25	26
27	28	29	30			

October
S	M	T	W	T	F	S
				1	2	3
4	5	6	7	8	9	10
11	12	13	14	15	16	17
18	19	20	21	22	23	24
25	26	27	28	29	30	31

November
S	M	T	W	T	F	S
1	2	3	4	5	6	7
8	9	10	11	12	13	14
15	16	17	18	19	20	21
22	23	24	25	26	27	28
29	30					

December
S	M	T	W	T	F	S
		1	2	3	4	5
6	7	8	9	10	11	12
13	14	15	16	17	18	19
20	21	22	23	24	25	26
27	28	29	30	31		

Year in Pixels

	J	F	M	A	M	J	J	A	S	O	N	D
1.												
2.												
3.												
4.												
5.												
6.												
7.												
8.												
9.												
10.												
11.												
12.												
13.												
14.												
15.												
16.												
17.												
18.												
19.												
20.												
21.												
22.												
23.												
24.												
25.												
26.												
27.												
28.												
29.												
30.												
31.												

Color Codes

Notes

January

MONDAY	TUESDAY	WEDNESDAY	THURSDAY
			1
5	6	7	8
12	13	14	15
19	20	21	22
26	27	28	29

January

FRIDAY	SATURDAY	SUNDAY	NOTES
2	3	4	○
			○
			○
			○
			○
9	10	11	○
			○
			○
			○
16	17	18	○
			○
			○
			○
			○
23	24	25	○
			○
			○
			○
			○
30	31		NOTES

February

MONDAY	TUESDAY	WEDNESDAY	THURSDAY
2	3	4	5
9	10	11	12
16	17	18	19
23	24	25	26

February

FRIDAY	SATURDAY	SUNDAY	NOTES
		1	○
			○
			○
			○
			○
6	7	8	○
			○
			○
			○
13	14	15	○
			○
			○
			○
			○
20	21	22	○
			○
			○
			○
			○
27	28		NOTES

March

MONDAY	TUESDAY	WEDNESDAY	THURSDAY
2	3	4	5
9	10	11	12
16	17	18	19
23	24	25	26

March

FRIDAY	SATURDAY	SUNDAY	NOTES
		1	○
			○
			○
			○
			○
6	7	8	○
			○
			○
			○
			○
13	14	15	○
			○
			○
			○
			○
20	21	22	○
			○
			○
			○
			○
27	28	29	30
			31

April 2026

MONDAY	TUESDAY	WEDNESDAY	THURSDAY
		1	2
6	7	8	9
13	14	15	16
20	21	22	23
27	28	29	30

April

FRIDAY	SATURDAY	SUNDAY	NOTES
3	4	5	○
			○
			○
			○
			○
10	11	12	○
			○
			○
			○
17	18	19	○
			○
			○
			○
			○
24	25	26	○
			○
			○
			○
			○
			NOTES

May 2026

MONDAY	TUESDAY	WEDNESDAY	THURSDAY
4	5	6	7
11	12	13	14
18	19	20	21
25	26	27	28

May 2026

FRIDAY	SATURDAY	SUNDAY	NOTES
1	2	3	○
			○
			○
			○
			○
8	9	10	○
			○
			○
			○
15	16	17	○
			○
			○
			○
			○
22	23	24	○
			○
			○
			○
			○
29	30	31	Notes

June

MONDAY	TUESDAY	WEDNESDAY	THURSDAY
1	2	3	4
8	9	10	11
15	16	17	18
22	23	24	25
29	30		

June

FRIDAY	SATURDAY	SUNDAY	NOTES
5	6	7	○
			○
			○
			○
			○
12	13	14	○
			○
			○
			○
19	20	21	○
			○
			○
			○
			○
26	27	28	○
			○
			○
			○
			○
			Notes

July

MONDAY	TUESDAY	WEDNESDAY	THURSDAY
		1	2
6	7	8	9
13	14	15	16
20	21	22	23
27	28	29	30

July

FRIDAY	SATURDAY	SUNDAY	NOTES
3	4	5	○
			○
			○
			○
			○
10	11	12	○
			○
			○
			○
17	18	19	○
			○
			○
			○
			○
24	25	26	○
			○
			○
			○
			○
31			NOTES

August 2026

MONDAY	TUESDAY	WEDNESDAY	THURSDAY
3	4	5	6
10	11	12	13
17	18	19	20
24	25	26	27

August

2026

FRIDAY	SATURDAY	SUNDAY	NOTES
	1	2	○
			○
			○
			○
			○
7	8	9	○
			○
			○
			○
14	15	16	○
			○
			○
			○
			○
21	22	23	○
			○
			○
			○
			○
28	29	30	31

September 2026

MONDAY	TUESDAY	WEDNESDAY	THURSDAY
	1	2	3
7	8	9	10
14	15	16	17
21	22	23	24
28	29	30	

September 2026

FRIDAY	SATURDAY	SUNDAY	NOTES
4	5	6	○
			○
			○
			○
			○
11	12	13	○
			○
			○
			○
18	19	20	○
			○
			○
			○
			○
25	26	27	○
			○
			○
			○
			○
			NOTES

October 2026

MONDAY	TUESDAY	WEDNESDAY	THURSDAY
			1
5	6	7	8
12	13	14	15
19	20	21	22
26	27	28	29

October

FRIDAY	SATURDAY	SUNDAY	NOTES
2	3	4	○
			○
			○
			○
			○
9	10	11	○
			○
			○
			○
16	17	18	○
			○
			○
			○
			○
23	24	25	○
			○
			○
			○
			○
30	31		NOTES

November $\qquad$ 2026

MONDAY	TUESDAY	WEDNESDAY	THURSDAY
2	3	4	5
9	10	11	12
16	17	18	19
23	24	25	26

November 2026

FRIDAY	SATURDAY	SUNDAY	NOTES
		1	○
			○
			○
			○
6	7	8	○
			○
			○
			○
			○
13	14	15	○
			○
			○
			○
			○
20	21	22	○
			○
			○
			○
			○
27	28	29	30

December

MONDAY	TUESDAY	WEDNESDAY	THURSDAY
	1	2	3
7	8	9	10
14	15	16	17
21	22	23	24
28	29	30	31

December 2026

FRIDAY	SATURDAY	SUNDAY	NOTES
4	5	6	○
			○
			○
			○
			○
11	12	13	○
			○
			○
			○
18	19	20	○
			○
			○
			○
			○
25	26	27	○
			○
			○
			○
			○
			NOTES

01 MONDAY

○ _____
○ _____
○ _____
○ _____
○ _____
○ _____
○ _____
○ _____

02 TUESDAY

○ _____
○ _____
○ _____
○ _____
○ _____
○ _____
○ _____
○ _____

03 WEDNESDAY

○ _____
○ _____
○ _____
○ _____
○ _____
○ _____
○ _____
○ _____

04 FRIDAY

○ _____
○ _____
○ _____
○ _____
○ _____

December
2025

05 FRIDAY

○ _____
○ _____
○ _____
○ _____
○ _____
○ _____
○ _____
○ _____

06 SATURDAY

○ _____
○ _____
○ _____
○ _____
○ _____
○ _____
○ _____
○ _____

07 SUNDAY

○ _____
○ _____
○ _____
○ _____
○ _____
○ _____
○ _____
○ _____

08 MONDAY

○ _____
○ _____
○ _____
○ _____
○ _____

09 TUESDAY

10 WEDNESDAY

11 THURSDAY

12 FRIDAY

December
2025

13 SATURDAY

○
○
○
○
○
○
○
○

14 SUNDAY

○
○
○
○
○
○
○
○
○

15 MONDAY

○
○
○
○
○
○
○
○

16 TUESDAY

○
○
○
○
○

17 WEDNESDAY

○ _____
○ _____
○ _____
○ _____
○ _____
○ _____
○ _____
○ _____

18 THURSDAY

○ _____
○ _____
○ _____
○ _____
○ _____
○ _____
○ _____
○ _____
○ _____

19 FRIDAY

○ _____
○ _____
○ _____
○ _____
○ _____
○ _____
○ _____
○ _____

20 SATURDAY

○ _____
○ _____
○ _____
○ _____
○ _____

21 SUNDAY

○
○
○
○
○
○
○
○

22 MONDAY

○
○
○
○
○
○
○
○
○

23 TUESDAY

○
○
○
○
○
○
○
○

24 WEDNESDAY

○
○
○
○
○

25 THURSDAY

○ _____
○ _____
○ _____
○ _____
○ _____
○ _____
○ _____
○ _____

26 FRIDAY

○ _____
○ _____
○ _____
○ _____
○ _____
○ _____
○ _____
○ _____

27 SATURDAY

○ _____
○ _____
○ _____
○ _____
○ _____
○ _____
○ _____
○ _____

28 SUNDAY

○ _____
○ _____
○ _____
○ _____
○ _____

29 MONDAY

○
○
○
○
○
○
○
○

30 TUESDAY

○
○
○
○
○
○
○
○

31 WEDNESDAY

○
○
○
○
○
○
○
○

NOTES

January
2026

01 THURSDAY

- _____
- _____
- _____
- _____
- _____
- _____
- _____
- _____

02 FRIDAY

- _____
- _____
- _____
- _____
- _____
- _____
- _____
- _____

03 SATURDAY

- _____
- _____
- _____
- _____
- _____
- _____
- _____
- _____

04 SUNDAY

- _____
- _____
- _____
- _____
- _____

05 MONDAY

○
○
○
○
○
○
○
○

06 TUESDAY

○
○
○
○
○
○
○
○

07 WEDNESDAY

○
○
○
○
○
○
○
○

08 THURSDAY

○
○
○
○
○

09 FRIDAY

○ _____
○ _____
○ _____
○ _____
○ _____
○ _____
○ _____
○ _____

10 SATURDAY

○ _____
○ _____
○ _____
○ _____
○ _____
○ _____
○ _____
○ _____

11 SUNDAY

○ _____
○ _____
○ _____
○ _____
○ _____
○ _____
○ _____
○ _____

12 MONDAY

○ _____
○ _____
○ _____
○ _____
○ _____

13 TUESDAY

○
○
○
○
○
○
○
○

14 WEDNESDAY

○
○
○
○
○
○
○
○
○

15 THURSDAY

○
○
○
○
○
○
○
○

16 FRIDAY

○
○
○
○
○

January
2026

17 SATURDAY

○ _____
○ _____
○ _____
○ _____
○ _____
○ _____
○ _____
○ _____

18 SUNDAY

○ _____
○ _____
○ _____
○ _____
○ _____
○ _____
○ _____
○ _____

19 MONDAY

○ _____
○ _____
○ _____
○ _____
○ _____
○ _____
○ _____
○ _____

20 TUESDAY

○ _____
○ _____
○ _____
○ _____
○ _____

21 WEDNESDAY

○
○
○
○
○
○
○
○

22 THURSDAY

○
○
○
○
○
○
○
○
○

23 FRIDAY

○
○
○
○
○
○
○
○

24 SATURDAY

○
○
○
○
○

25 SUNDAY

○ _____
○ _____
○ _____
○ _____
○ _____
○ _____
○ _____
○ _____

26 MONDAY

○ _____
○ _____
○ _____
○ _____
○ _____
○ _____
○ _____
○ _____

27 TUESDAY

○ _____
○ _____
○ _____
○ _____
○ _____
○ _____
○ _____
○ _____

28 WEDNESDAY

○ _____
○ _____
○ _____
○ _____
○ _____

29 THURSDAY

○ _____
○ _____
○ _____
○ _____
○ _____
○ _____
○ _____
○ _____

30 FRIDAY

○ _____
○ _____
○ _____
○ _____
○ _____
○ _____
○ _____
○ _____

31 SATURDAY

○ _____
○ _____
○ _____
○ _____
○ _____
○ _____
○ _____
○ _____

NOTES

_____
_____
_____
_____

February 2026

01 SUNDAY

02 MONDAY

03 TUESDAY

04 WEDNESDAY

05 THURSDAY

○
○
○
○
○
○
○
○

06 FRIDAY

○
○
○
○
○
○
○
○

07 SATURDAY

○
○
○
○
○
○
○
○

08 SUNDAY

○
○
○
○
○

09 MONDAY
- ○ _____
- ○ _____
- ○ _____
- ○ _____
- ○ _____
- ○ _____
- ○ _____
- ○ _____

10 TUESDAY
- ○ _____
- ○ _____
- ○ _____
- ○ _____
- ○ _____
- ○ _____
- ○ _____
- ○ _____

11 WEDNESDAY
- ○ _____
- ○ _____
- ○ _____
- ○ _____
- ○ _____
- ○ _____
- ○ _____
- ○ _____

12 THURSDAY
- ○ _____
- ○ _____
- ○ _____
- ○ _____
- ○ _____

13 FRIDAY

○
○
○
○
○
○
○
○

14 SATURDAY

○
○
○
○
○
○
○
○

15 SUNDAY

○
○
○
○
○
○
○
○

16 MONDAY

○
○
○
○
○

17 TUESDAY

18 WEDNESDAY

19 THURSDAY

20 FRIDAY

21 SATURDAY
○
○
○
○
○
○
○
○

22 SUNDAY
○
○
○
○
○
○
○
○
○

23 MONDAY
○
○
○
○
○
○
○
○

24 TUESDAY
○
○
○
○
○

25 WEDNESDAY

○
○
○
○
○
○
○
○

26 THURSDAY

○
○
○
○
○
○
○
○

27 FRIDAY

○
○
○
○
○
○
○
○

28 SATURDAY

○
○
○
○
○

March 2026

01 SUNDAY

○ _____
○ _____
○ _____
○ _____
○ _____
○ _____
○ _____
○ _____

02 MONDAY

○ _____
○ _____
○ _____
○ _____
○ _____
○ _____
○ _____
○ _____

03 TUESDAY

○ _____
○ _____
○ _____
○ _____
○ _____
○ _____
○ _____
○ _____

04 WEDNESDAY

○ _____
○ _____
○ _____
○ _____
○ _____

05 THURSDAY

- ○ _____
- ○ _____
- ○ _____
- ○ _____
- ○ _____
- ○ _____
- ○ _____
- ○ _____

06 FRIDAY

- ○ _____
- ○ _____
- ○ _____
- ○ _____
- ○ _____
- ○ _____
- ○ _____
- ○ _____

07 SATURDAY

- ○ _____
- ○ _____
- ○ _____
- ○ _____
- ○ _____
- ○ _____
- ○ _____
- ○ _____

08 SUNDAY

- ○ _____
- ○ _____
- ○ _____
- ○ _____
- ○ _____

March 2026

09 MONDAY

10 TUESDAY

11 WEDNESDAY

12 THURSDAY

13 FRIDAY

○ _____
○ _____
○ _____
○ _____
○ _____
○ _____
○ _____
○ _____

14 SATURDAY

○ _____
○ _____
○ _____
○ _____
○ _____
○ _____
○ _____
○ _____

15 SUNDAY

○ _____
○ _____
○ _____
○ _____
○ _____
○ _____
○ _____
○ _____

16 MONDAY

○ _____
○ _____
○ _____
○ _____
○ _____

17 TUESDAY

18 WEDNESDAY

19 THURSDAY

20 FRIDAY

21 SATURDAY

○ _____
○ _____
○ _____
○ _____
○ _____
○ _____
○ _____
○ _____

22 SUNDAY

○ _____
○ _____
○ _____
○ _____
○ _____
○ _____
○ _____
○ _____

23 MONDAY

○ _____
○ _____
○ _____
○ _____
○ _____
○ _____
○ _____
○ _____

24 TUESDAY

○ _____
○ _____
○ _____
○ _____
○ _____

March
2026

25 WEDNESDAY

26 THURSDAY

27 FRIDAY

28 SATURDAY

29 SUNDAY

- ○
- ○
- ○
- ○
- ○
- ○
- ○
- ○

30 MONDAY

- ○
- ○
- ○
- ○
- ○
- ○
- ○
- ○

31 TUESDAY

- ○
- ○
- ○
- ○
- ○
- ○
- ○
- ○

NOTES

April
2026

01 WEDNESDAY

○
○
○
○
○
○
○
○

02 THURSDAY

○
○
○
○
○
○
○
○

03 FRIDAY

○
○
○
○
○
○
○
○

04 SATURDAY

○
○
○
○
○

April
2026

05 SUNDAY

○ _____
○ _____
○ _____
○ _____
○ _____
○ _____
○ _____
○ _____

06 MONDAY

○ _____
○ _____
○ _____
○ _____
○ _____
○ _____
○ _____
○ _____

07 TUESDAY

○ _____
○ _____
○ _____
○ _____
○ _____
○ _____
○ _____
○ _____

08 WEDNESDAY

○ _____
○ _____
○ _____
○ _____
○ _____

09 THURSDAY

○
○
○
○
○
○
○
○

10 FRIDAY

○
○
○
○
○
○
○
○

11 SATURDAY

○
○
○
○
○
○
○
○

12 SUNDAY

○
○
○
○
○

13 MONDAY

○
○
○
○
○
○
○
○

14 TUESDAY

○
○
○
○
○
○
○
○

15 WEDNESDAY

○
○
○
○
○
○
○
○

16 THURSDAY

○
○
○
○
○

17 FRIDAY

○
○
○
○
○
○
○
○

18 SATURDAY

○
○
○
○
○
○
○
○

19 SUNDAY

○
○
○
○
○
○
○
○

20 MONDAY

○
○
○
○
○

21 TUESDAY

○ _____
○ _____
○ _____
○ _____
○ _____
○ _____
○ _____
○ _____

22 WEDNESDAY

○ _____
○ _____
○ _____
○ _____
○ _____
○ _____
○ _____
○ _____

23 THURSDAY

○ _____
○ _____
○ _____
○ _____
○ _____
○ _____
○ _____
○ _____

24 FRIDAY

○ _____
○ _____
○ _____
○ _____
○ _____

25 SATURDAY

○
○
○
○
○
○
○
○

26 SUNDAY

○
○
○
○
○
○
○
○

27 MONDAY

○
○
○
○
○
○
○
○

28 TUESDAY

○
○
○
○
○

29 WEDNESDAY

○ _____
○ _____
○ _____
○ _____
○ _____
○ _____
○ _____
○ _____

30 THURSDAY

○ _____
○ _____
○ _____
○ _____
○ _____
○ _____
○ _____
○ _____

NOTES

_____
_____
_____
_____
_____
_____
_____
_____
_____
_____
_____
_____

May
2026

01 FRIDAY
○
○
○
○
○
○
○
○

02 SATURDAY
○
○
○
○
○
○
○
○

03 SUNDAY
○
○
○
○
○
○
○
○

04 MONDAY
○
○
○
○
○

May
2026

05 TUESDAY

06 WEDNESDAY

07 THURSDAY

08 FRIDAY

09 SATURDAY

○
○
○
○
○
○
○
○

10 SUNDAY

○
○
○
○
○
○
○
○

11 MONDAY

○
○
○
○
○
○
○
○

12 TUESDAY

○
○
○
○
○

13 WEDNESDAY
○
○
○
○
○
○
○
○

14 THURSDAY
○
○
○
○
○
○
○
○

15 FRIDAY
○
○
○
○
○
○
○
○

16 SATURDAY
○
○
○
○
○

17 SUNDAY

○
○
○
○
○
○
○
○

18 MONDAY

○
○
○
○
○
○
○
○

19 TUESDAY

○
○
○
○
○
○
○
○

20 WEDNESDAY

○
○
○
○
○

21 THURSDAY

22 FRIDAY

23 SATURDAY

24 SUNDAY

May 2026

25 MONDAY

○
○
○
○
○
○
○
○

26 TUESDAY

○
○
○
○
○
○
○
○

27 WEDNESDAY

○
○
○
○
○
○
○
○

28 THURSDAY

○
○
○
○
○

29 FRIDAY

○ _____
○ _____
○ _____
○ _____
○ _____
○ _____
○ _____
○ _____

30 SATURDAY

○ _____
○ _____
○ _____
○ _____
○ _____
○ _____
○ _____
○ _____

31 SUNDAY

○ _____
○ _____
○ _____
○ _____
○ _____
○ _____
○ _____
○ _____

NOTES

_____
_____
_____
_____
_____

01 MONDAY

○
○
○
○
○
○
○
○

02 TUESDAY

○
○
○
○
○
○
○
○

03 WEDNESDAY

○
○
○
○
○
○
○
○

04 THURSDAY

○
○
○
○
○

05 FRIDAY

○ _____
○ _____
○ _____
○ _____
○ _____
○ _____
○ _____
○ _____

06 SATURDAY

○ _____
○ _____
○ _____
○ _____
○ _____
○ _____
○ _____
○ _____

07 SUNDAY

○ _____
○ _____
○ _____
○ _____
○ _____
○ _____
○ _____
○ _____

08 MONDAY

○ _____
○ _____
○ _____
○ _____
○ _____

09 TUESDAY

○
○
○
○
○
○
○
○

10 WEDNESDAY

○
○
○
○
○
○
○
○

11 THURSDAY

○
○
○
○
○
○
○
○

12 FRIDAY

○
○
○
○
○

13 SATURDAY

○
○
○
○
○
○
○
○

14 SUNDAY

○
○
○
○
○
○
○
○

15 MONDAY

○
○
○
○
○
○
○
○

16 TUESDAY

○
○
○
○
○

17 WEDNESDAY

○
○
○
○
○
○
○
○

18 THURSDAY

○
○
○
○
○
○
○
○

19 FRIDAY

○
○
○
○
○
○
○
○

20 SATURDAY

○
○
○
○
○

21 SUNDAY

22 MONDAY

23 TUESDAY

24 WEDNESDAY

25 THURSDAY

○
○
○
○
○
○
○
○

26 FRIDAY

○
○
○
○
○
○
○
○

27 SATURDAY

○
○
○
○
○
○
○
○

28 SUNDAY

○
○
○
○
○

29 MONDAY

○
○
○
○
○
○
○
○

30 TUESDAY

○
○
○
○
○
○
○
○

NOTES

July
2026

01 WEDNESDAY
○
○
○
○
○
○
○
○

02 THURSDAY
○
○
○
○
○
○
○
○

03 FRIDAY
○
○
○
○
○
○
○
○

04 SATURDAY
○
○
○
○
○

05 SUNDAY
- ○
- ○
- ○
- ○
- ○
- ○
- ○
- ○

06 MONDAY
- ○
- ○
- ○
- ○
- ○
- ○
- ○
- ○

07 TUESDAY
- ○
- ○
- ○
- ○
- ○
- ○
- ○
- ○

08 WEDNESDAY
- ○
- ○
- ○
- ○
- ○

July
2026

09 THURSDAY
○
○
○
○
○
○
○
○

10 FRIDAY
○
○
○
○
○
○
○
○

11 SATURDAY
○
○
○
○
○
○
○
○

12 SUNDAY
○
○
○
○
○

13 MONDAY

○
○
○
○
○
○
○
○

14 TUESDAY

○
○
○
○
○
○
○
○

15 WEDNESDAY

○
○
○
○
○
○
○
○

16 THURSDAY

○
○
○
○
○

17 FRIDAY
○
○
○
○
○
○
○
○

18 SATURDAY
○
○
○
○
○
○
○
○

19 SUNDAY
○
○
○
○
○
○
○
○

20 MONDAY
○
○
○
○
○

21 TUESDAY

○ _____
○ _____
○ _____
○ _____
○ _____
○ _____
○ _____
○ _____

22 WEDNESDAY

○ _____
○ _____
○ _____
○ _____
○ _____
○ _____
○ _____
○ _____

23 THURSDAY

○ _____
○ _____
○ _____
○ _____
○ _____
○ _____
○ _____
○ _____

24 FRIDAY

○ _____
○ _____
○ _____
○ _____
○ _____

25 SATURDAY

26 SUNDAY

27 MONDAY

28 TUESDAY

29 WEDNESDAY

- ○
- ○
- ○
- ○
- ○
- ○
- ○
- ○

30 THURSDAY

- ○
- ○
- ○
- ○
- ○
- ○
- ○
- ○

31 FRIDAY

- ○
- ○
- ○
- ○
- ○
- ○
- ○
- ○

NOTES

August
2026

01 SATURDAY
○
○
○
○
○
○
○
○

02 SUNDAY
○
○
○
○
○
○
○
○

03 MONDAY
○
○
○
○
○
○
○
○

04 TUESDAY
○
○
○
○
○

05 WEDNESDAY

○ _____
○ _____
○ _____
○ _____
○ _____
○ _____
○ _____
○ _____

06 THURSDAY

○ _____
○ _____
○ _____
○ _____
○ _____
○ _____
○ _____
○ _____

07 FRIDAY

○ _____
○ _____
○ _____
○ _____
○ _____
○ _____
○ _____
○ _____

08 SATURDAY

○ _____
○ _____
○ _____
○ _____
○ _____

August
2026

09 SUNDAY
- ○
- ○
- ○
- ○
- ○
- ○
- ○
- ○

10 MONDAY
- ○
- ○
- ○
- ○
- ○
- ○
- ○
- ○

11 TUESDAY
- ○
- ○
- ○
- ○
- ○
- ○
- ○
- ○

12 WEDNESDAY
- ○
- ○
- ○
- ○
- ○

13 THURSDAY

○ _____
○ _____
○ _____
○ _____
○ _____
○ _____
○ _____
○ _____

14 FRIDAY

○ _____
○ _____
○ _____
○ _____
○ _____
○ _____
○ _____
○ _____

15 SATURDAY

○ _____
○ _____
○ _____
○ _____
○ _____
○ _____
○ _____
○ _____

16 SUNDAY

○ _____
○ _____
○ _____
○ _____
○ _____

17 MONDAY

○ _____
○ _____
○ _____
○ _____
○ _____
○ _____
○ _____
○ _____

18 TUESDAY

○ _____
○ _____
○ _____
○ _____
○ _____
○ _____
○ _____
○ _____

19 WEDNESDAY

○ _____
○ _____
○ _____
○ _____
○ _____
○ _____
○ _____
○ _____

20 THURSDAY

○ _____
○ _____
○ _____
○ _____
○ _____

21 FRIDAY

-
-
-
-
-
-
-

22 SATURDAY

-
-
-
-
-
-
-
-

23 SUNDAY

-
-
-
-
-
-
-
-

24 MONDAY

-
-
-
-
-

25 TUESDAY
○
○
○
○
○
○
○
○

26 WEDNESDAY
○
○
○
○
○
○
○
○
○

27 THURSDAY
○
○
○
○
○
○
○
○

28 FRIDAY
○
○
○
○
○

August
2026

29 SATURDAY

○ _____
○ _____
○ _____
○ _____
○ _____
○ _____
○ _____
○ _____

30 SUNDAY

○ _____
○ _____
○ _____
○ _____
○ _____
○ _____
○ _____
○ _____

31 MONDAY

○ _____
○ _____
○ _____
○ _____
○ _____
○ _____
○ _____
○ _____

NOTES

_____
_____
_____
_____

01 TUESDAY

○
○
○
○
○
○
○
○

02 WEDNESDAY

○
○
○
○
○
○
○
○

03 THURSDAY

○
○
○
○
○
○
○
○

04 FRIDAY

○
○
○
○
○

05 SATURDAY

○ _____
○ _____
○ _____
○ _____
○ _____
○ _____
○ _____
○ _____

06 SUNDAY

○ _____
○ _____
○ _____
○ _____
○ _____
○ _____
○ _____
○ _____

07 MONDAY

○ _____
○ _____
○ _____
○ _____
○ _____
○ _____
○ _____
○ _____

08 TUESDAY

○ _____
○ _____
○ _____
○ _____
○ _____

09 WEDNESDAY

10 THURSDAY

11 FRIDAY

12 SATURDAY

13 SUNDAY

○ _____
○ _____
○ _____
○ _____
○ _____
○ _____
○ _____
○ _____

14 MONDAY

○ _____
○ _____
○ _____
○ _____
○ _____
○ _____
○ _____
○ _____

15 TUESDAY

○ _____
○ _____
○ _____
○ _____
○ _____
○ _____
○ _____
○ _____

16 WEDNESDAY

○ _____
○ _____
○ _____
○ _____
○ _____

17 THURSDAY

○
○
○
○
○
○
○
○

18 FRIDAY

○
○
○
○
○
○
○
○

19 SATURDAY

○
○
○
○
○
○
○
○

20 SUNDAY

○
○
○
○
○

21 MONDAY

○ _____
○ _____
○ _____
○ _____
○ _____
○ _____
○ _____
○ _____

22 TUESDAY

○ _____
○ _____
○ _____
○ _____
○ _____
○ _____
○ _____
○ _____

23 WEDNESDAY

○ _____
○ _____
○ _____
○ _____
○ _____
○ _____
○ _____
○ _____

24 THURSDAY

○ _____
○ _____
○ _____
○ _____
○ _____

25 FRIDAY

○
○
○
○
○
○
○
○

26 SATURDAY

○
○
○
○
○
○
○
○
○

27 SUNDAY

○
○
○
○
○
○
○
○

28 MONDAY

○
○
○
○
○

29 TUESDAY

- ○ _____
- ○ _____
- ○ _____
- ○ _____
- ○ _____
- ○ _____
- ○ _____
- ○ _____

30 WEDNESDAY

- ○ _____
- ○ _____
- ○ _____
- ○ _____
- ○ _____
- ○ _____
- ○ _____
- ○ _____

NOTES

_____
_____
_____
_____
_____
_____
_____
_____
_____
_____
_____
_____
_____

October
2026

01 THURSDAY

○
○
○
○
○
○
○
○

02 FRIDAY

○
○
○
○
○
○
○
○

03 SATURDAY

○
○
○
○
○
○
○
○

04 SUNDAY

○
○
○
○
○

05 MONDAY

○ _____
○ _____
○ _____
○ _____
○ _____
○ _____
○ _____
○ _____

06 TUESDAY

○ _____
○ _____
○ _____
○ _____
○ _____
○ _____
○ _____
○ _____

07 WEDNESDAY

○ _____
○ _____
○ _____
○ _____
○ _____
○ _____
○ _____
○ _____

08 THURSDAY

○ _____
○ _____
○ _____
○ _____
○ _____

09 FRIDAY

○
○
○
○
○
○
○
○

10 SATURDAY

○
○
○
○
○
○
○
○
○

11 SUNDAY

○
○
○
○
○
○
○
○

12 MONDAY

○
○
○
○
○

13 TUESDAY

○ _____
○ _____
○ _____
○ _____
○ _____
○ _____
○ _____
○ _____

14 WEDNESDAY

○ _____
○ _____
○ _____
○ _____
○ _____
○ _____
○ _____
○ _____

15 THURSDAY

○ _____
○ _____
○ _____
○ _____
○ _____
○ _____
○ _____
○ _____

16 FRIDAY

○ _____
○ _____
○ _____
○ _____
○ _____

17 SATURDAY

18 SUNDAY

19 MONDAY

20 TUESDAY

21 WEDNESDAY
- ○
- ○
- ○
- ○
- ○
- ○
- ○
- ○

22 THURSDAY
- ○
- ○
- ○
- ○
- ○
- ○
- ○
- ○

23 FRIDAY
- ○
- ○
- ○
- ○
- ○
- ○
- ○
- ○

24 SATURDAY
- ○
- ○
- ○
- ○
- ○

October
2026

25 SUNDAY

26 MONDAY

27 TUESDAY

28 WEDNESDAY

29 THURSDAY

○ _____
○ _____
○ _____
○ _____
○ _____
○ _____
○ _____
○ _____

30 FRIDAY

○ _____
○ _____
○ _____
○ _____
○ _____
○ _____
○ _____
○ _____

31 SATURDAY

○ _____
○ _____
○ _____
○ _____
○ _____
○ _____
○ _____
○ _____

NOTES

_____
_____
_____
_____

November
2026

01 SUNDAY

○
○
○
○
○
○
○
○

02 MONDAY

○
○
○
○
○
○
○
○

03 TUESDAY

○
○
○
○
○
○
○
○

04 WEDNESDAY

○
○
○
○
○

05 THURSDAY

○ _____
○ _____
○ _____
○ _____
○ _____
○ _____
○ _____
○ _____

06 FRIDAY

○ _____
○ _____
○ _____
○ _____
○ _____
○ _____
○ _____
○ _____

07 SATURDAY

○ _____
○ _____
○ _____
○ _____
○ _____
○ _____
○ _____
○ _____

08 SUNDAY

○ _____
○ _____
○ _____
○ _____
○ _____

November
2026

09 MONDAY

○
○
○
○
○
○
○
○

10 TUESDAY

○
○
○
○
○
○
○
○

11 WEDNESDAY

○
○
○
○
○
○
○
○

12 THURSDAY

○
○
○
○
○

November
2026

13 FRIDAY

○ _____
○ _____
○ _____
○ _____
○ _____
○ _____
○ _____
○ _____

14 SATURDAY

○ _____
○ _____
○ _____
○ _____
○ _____
○ _____
○ _____
○ _____

15 SUNDAY

○ _____
○ _____
○ _____
○ _____
○ _____
○ _____
○ _____
○ _____

16 MONDAY

○ _____
○ _____
○ _____
○ _____
○ _____

17 TUESDAY

○
○
○
○
○
○
○
○

18 WEDNESDAY

○
○
○
○
○
○
○
○

19 THURSDAY

○
○
○
○
○
○
○
○

20 FRIDAY

○
○
○
○
○

November
2026

21 SATURDAY

○ _____
○ _____
○ _____
○ _____
○ _____
○ _____
○ _____
○ _____

22 SUNDAY

○ _____
○ _____
○ _____
○ _____
○ _____
○ _____
○ _____
○ _____

23 MONDAY

○ _____
○ _____
○ _____
○ _____
○ _____
○ _____
○ _____
○ _____

24 TUESDAY

○ _____
○ _____
○ _____
○ _____
○ _____

November
2026

25 WEDNESDAY
- ○
- ○
- ○
- ○
- ○
- ○
- ○
- ○

26 THURSDAY
- ○
- ○
- ○
- ○
- ○
- ○
- ○
- ○

27 FRIDAY
- ○
- ○
- ○
- ○
- ○
- ○
- ○
- ○

28 SATURDAY
- ○
- ○
- ○
- ○
- ○

29 SUNDAY

○ _____
○ _____
○ _____
○ _____
○ _____
○ _____
○ _____
○ _____

30 MONDAY

○ _____
○ _____
○ _____
○ _____
○ _____
○ _____
○ _____
○ _____

NOTES

_____
_____
_____
_____
_____
_____
_____
_____
_____
_____
_____
_____
_____

December
2026

01 TUESDAY

○ _____
○ _____
○ _____
○ _____
○ _____
○ _____
○ _____
○ _____

02 WEDNESDAY

○ _____
○ _____
○ _____
○ _____
○ _____
○ _____
○ _____
○ _____

03 THURSDAY

○ _____
○ _____
○ _____
○ _____
○ _____
○ _____
○ _____
○ _____

04 FRIDAY

○ _____
○ _____
○ _____
○ _____
○ _____

05 SATURDAY

06 SUNDAY

07 MONDAY

08 TUESDAY

December
2026

09 WEDNESDAY
- ○
- ○
- ○
- ○
- ○
- ○
- ○
- ○

10 THURSDAY
- ○
- ○
- ○
- ○
- ○
- ○
- ○
- ○

11 FRIDAY
- ○
- ○
- ○
- ○
- ○
- ○
- ○
- ○

12 SATURDAY
- ○
- ○
- ○
- ○
- ○

13 SUNDAY

14 MONDAY

15 TUESDAY

16 WEDNESDAY

17 THURSDAY

○
○
○
○
○
○
○
○

18 FRIDAY

○
○
○
○
○
○
○
○

19 SATURDAY

○
○
○
○
○
○
○
○

20 SUNDAY

○
○
○
○
○

21 MONDAY

○ _____
○ _____
○ _____
○ _____
○ _____
○ _____
○ _____
○ _____

22 TUESDAY

○ _____
○ _____
○ _____
○ _____
○ _____
○ _____
○ _____
○ _____

23 WEDNESDAY

○ _____
○ _____
○ _____
○ _____
○ _____
○ _____
○ _____
○ _____

24 THURSDAY

○ _____
○ _____
○ _____
○ _____
○ _____

December
2026

25 FRIDAY

○
○
○
○
○
○
○
○

26 SATURDAY

○
○
○
○
○
○
○
○
○

27 SUNDAY

○
○
○
○
○
○
○
○

28 MONDAY

○
○
○
○
○

29 TUESDAY

- ○
- ○
- ○
- ○
- ○
- ○
- ○
- ○

30 WEDNESDAY

- ○
- ○
- ○
- ○
- ○
- ○
- ○
- ○

31 THURSDAY

- ○
- ○
- ○
- ○
- ○
- ○
- ○
- ○

NOTES

www.ingramcontent.com/pod-product-compliance
Lightning Source LLC
Chambersburg PA
CBHW052113020426

42335CB00021B/2749